Bats, Brownies & Banana Bread:
The Library Bats' Bakery (and More) Recipe Book

Illustrations and Design: Maureen Heidtmann

Drowsy Duck Publications
117 Collie Brook Road,
East Hampton, CT 06424

Printed in the United States of America ISBN: 9781091985292

This book is dedicated to Elvira, Quigly, Pugsly and Eric - some of the bats I have known - and to my friends and family for their support and understanding.

"Every day is Halloween at my house."
- Cosmos Heidtmann (age 16 at the time of the quote)

About Maureen: I am a state licensed wildlife caretaker who specializes in bats, and a Certified Wildlife Conservationist. I have a permit from USDA to keep non-releasable bats to exhibit for educational purposes, and over the past 25 years I have presented programs to educate the public about bats: wonderful, beneficial, misunderstood and undervalued creatures.

All recipes include fruits, spices, nuts and other ingredients that depend on bats for pollination, seed dispersal and/or pest control. The recipes were contributed by patrons of East Haddam Free Public Library, Moodus, Connecticut and friends and family.

The idea for the book was inspired by bat connection recipes found in BATS Magazine: Bat Conservation International, Austin, Texas.

Bats, Brownies and Banana Bread: *The Library Bats' Bakery (and More) Book*

Did you know that over 500 plant species rely on bats to pollinate their flowers? These include species of banana and cocoa.
So, next time you eat chocolate brownies or banana bread, say 'thanks' to the bats!

Other kinds of bats eat the bugs that eat fruit nuts and spices, including oranges and pineapple, almonds and pistachios, ginger and cloves.
They also control insect pests that eat veggies, including tomatoes, squash and peppers.

Fun Bat Fact: The pollination of plants by bats is called *chiropterophily.*

Bats: Plant Pals from A to Z

The following food items rely on bats - naturally:

Agave, Allspice, Almonds, Apples, Artichokes, Asparagus, Avacado, Banana, Basil, Brazil nuts, Barley, Berries , Beets, Beans, Bok Choy, Brocolli, Brussells Sprouts, Carrots, Cauliflower, Cabbage, Cashews, Celery, Cherries, Citrus fruits, Cloves, Cocoa, Coconut, Coffee, Corn, Cucumber, Dates, Durian, Eggplant, Figs, Flax, Garlic, Ginger, Grapes, Guava, Hazelnuts, Hops, Kale, Lettuce, Mango, Mushrooms, Oats, Okra, Olives, Papaya, Peaches, Pears, Peanuts, Pecans, Peppercorns, Peppers, Peas, Pistachios, Plantains, Potatoes, Pumpkin, Radish, Rice, Rye, Sesame seeds, Spinach, Squash, Sugar Cane, Tomatoes, Vanilla, Vegetable oils, Walnuts, Wheat, Zucchini.

Many non-edible items such as soap, toothpaste and twine, have a bat connection too!

Wow!

Without bats, our shopping carts would be pretty empty!

Without bats, the pages in this book would be blank.

Many kinds of plants rely on bats for pollination.

Many kinds of plants rely on bats for pest control.

Many kinds of plants rely on bats to disperse seeds.

Many plants rely on bats for one, two or all three.

Introduction
Bats: Plant Pals
Meet the Library Bats
Fun Bat Facts

Joe R's Baklava Cake

Bake at 350 degrees for 30 minutes
Makes about 2 dozen squares
Honey Syrup (recipe follows)

1 ½ cups all-purpose flour
2 teaspoons baking powder
1 teaspoon ground cinnamon
¼ teaspoon salt
1 cup (2 sticks) butter or margarine softened
1 cup sugar
4 eggs
1 tablespoon grated orange rind
1/3 cup orange juice
2 cups finely chopped walnuts

1. Prepare and cool honey syrup
2. Sift flour, baking powder, cinnamon and salt onto wax paper. Butter a 13x9x2 inch pan. Preheat oven to 350.
3. Beat butter and sugar in a large bowl until well blended. Beat in eggs one at a time until mixture is light and fluffy. Stir in orange rind.
4. Stir in flour mixture alternately with orange juice, beating after each addition until batter is smooth. Stir in walnuts. Pour into prepared pan.
5. Bake for 30 minutes or until center springs back when lightly pressed with fingertip.
6. Cool cake in pan on wire rack 10 minutes; gradually pour syrup over cake, letting syrup soak in before adding more. Or cool cake completely, then pour hot syrup over cake.
7. To serve: Cut cake into 2 inch squares. Garnish each square with walnuts.

Honey Syrup: Combine one 2-inch piece orange rind, ½ cup sugar, ½ cup water and one 1 inch piece stick cinnamon. Bring to boil. Lower heat and simmer for 25 minutes or to 230 degrees on a candy thermometer. Stir in ½ cup honey. Remove rind and cinnamon stick. Cool.

> Fun Bat Fact: Bats don't make honey, but some bats eat bugs that eat bees! Insectivorous bats also prey on bugs that eat the flowers bees need to make honey. Sweet!

Maureen's single-bowl brownie recipe

1 pkg. (4 oz.) Unsweetened Chocolate
3/4 cup butter or margarine
2 cups sugar
3 eggs
1 tsp. vanilla
1 cup flour
1 cup coarsely chopped Pecans

Heat oven to 350°F. Butter a 9x9 inch pan.

Melt chocolate and butter in large bowl on low heat or micorwave on HIGH 2 min. or until butter is melted. Stir mixture. Stir in sugar. Blend in eggs and vanilla. Add flour and nuts; mix well. Pour into prepared buttered pan.
Bake 30 to 35 min. or until toothpick inserted in center comes out with fudgy crumbs. (Do not overbake.) Cool completely. Serve.

Fudgey Flour-free Brownies

8 oz. almond butter
1 egg
1 teaspoon vanilla extract
1/2 cup honey
1/3 cup unsweetened cocoa powder
1/2 teaspoon baking soda
1/4 teaspoon sea salt

Preheat oven to 325 degrees. Butter an 8x8 inch pan.

In a medium-sized bowl, beat almond butter until smooth and creamy. Add egg, vanilla, and honey, and beat until well mixed. Add cocoa powder, baking soda, and salt, and beat until well combined. Batter will be fairly thick.
Spread batter into prepared baking dish. Bake for 20 minutes, or until a toothpick inserted into the center comes out with a few moist crumbs.
Brownies are best when warm. Store covered at room temperature.

Fun Bat Fact: More than 500 plant species rely on bats to pollinate their flowers, including species of cocoa. Without bats there would be no brownies!

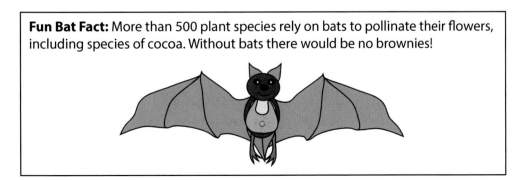

Amelia's Avacado Brownies

1/2 cup creamy nut butter (almond, cashew, tahini, etc)
1/2 cup chocolate chips
1/2 cup mashed avocado (about 1/2 an avocado)
1/2 cup cooked sweet potato
1/4 cup coconut milk
2 tablespoons maple syrup
3 tablespoons cacao powder

Preheat the oven to 325° F.
Grease a regular size loaf pan with coconut oil or line with parchment paper.
In a food processor or blender, combine all ingredients except chocolate chips and mix until well combined. Stir in the chocolate chips and transfer to the loaf pan. The batter will be very thick and sticky so with the back of a spoon, level out the batter across the pan as evenly as you can, edging it into the corners and smoothing the surface.
Bake for 20 minutes, then remove and allow to cool to before slicing

Almond Flour Brownies

2/3 cup honey
1/2 cup melted butter or coconut oil
1 Tbsp. vanilla extract
3 eggs
1 cup almond flour
1/2 cup cocoa (I used raw cacao)
1/4 tsp. baking soda (this can be omitted)
1/4 tsp. sea salt (omit if using salted butter)

Heat oven to 350 degrees F. Mix honey, butter, vanilla and eggs until smooth.
(If omitting baking soda, beat eggs until foamy before adding other wet ingredients.)
Add almond flour, cocoa, baking soda and salt. Stir to blend. Pour into greased 8x8x2" pan. Bake for approximately 25 minutes. Cool on a wire rack.

Fun Bat Fact: Many of our most valuable crops rely on bats for their survival, avocado included. Avocado flowers are pollinated by bats.

3

BB's Basic Banana Bread

2/3 cup sugar
1/3 cup shortening
2 cups all-purpose flour
2 teaspoons baking powder
1/4 teaspoon baking soda
1/4 teaspoon salt
1 cup mashed ripe bananas

In a large bowl, cream sugar and shortening for about 5 minutes (mixture does not get smooth). Combine flour, baking powder, baking soda and salt; add to creamed mixture alternately with bananas, beating after each addition (the batter will be thick). Spoon into a greased 9x5-in. loaf pan. Bake at 350° for 40-45 minutes or until bread tests done with a toothpick. Cool in pan for 10 minutes before removing to a wire rack. Yield: 1 loaf.

Zurie's Zucchini Banana Bread (makes 2 loaves)

3 cups all-purpose flour
1½ teaspoons baking powder
1½ teaspoons baking soda
1½ teaspoons ground cinnamon
1 teaspoon salt
4 eggs
2 cups granulated sugar
1 cup vegetable oil
2 medium ripe bananas, mashed (about 1 cup)
1½ cups shredded zucchini
1 cup chopped pecans

Preheat oven to 350 degrees. Grease two 9×5-inch loaf pans and set aside.
In a medium bowl, whisk together the flour, baking powder, baking soda, cinnamon and salt: set aside. In a large bowl, whisk the eggs. Add the sugar and oil and whisk until smooth. Whisk in the bananas and mix well. Add the flour mixture and stir with a rubber spatula until no flour remains. Fold in the zucchini and pecans. Divide the batter evenly between the two loaf pans. Bake until a toothpick inserted into the center comes out clean, 50 to 60 minutes. Cool on a wire rack for 10 minutes, then remove the bread from the pans and place on wire rack to cool completely.

Fun Bat Fact: Bats pollinate wild bananas and disperse their seeds. Commercial bananas are seedless and don't need pollination. However, the plants that produce all that fruit are so genetically similar that a single disease could wipe out the global crop, so it's important to keep healthy wild plants growing and producing fruit

Boris' Basic Banana Bread

3-4 ripe bananas (mashed)
1/3 cup melted butter
1 cup sugar
1 egg beaten
1 teaspoon vanilla extract
1 teaspoon baking soda
 pinch of salt
1 1/2 cups all purpose flour

Heat oven to 350. Mix butter and mashed bananas together. Add sugar, egg and vanilla. Add baking soda and salt and mix well. Add flour and give it a final mix. Pour into a greased 4 x 8 inch loaf pan. Bake for 1 hour. Cool and serve.

Whee! Wheat Free Banana Bread

3 bananas (mashed)
3 large eggs
1 tablespoon vanilla extract
1 tablespoon honey
¼ cup coconut shortening
2 cups blanched almond four
½ teaspoon sea salt
1 teaspoon baking soda

Pulse together bananas, eggs, vanilla, honey, and shortening in a food processor. Pulse in almond four, salt, and baking soda. Scoop batter into a greased 7.5 x 3.5 inch loaf pan. Bake at 350° for 55-65 minutes. Cool for 1 hour.

Sophie H's Molasses Pumpkin Pie

2 cups cooked pumpkin
1 1/2 cups condensed milk or rich cream
1/4 cup brown sugar
1/2 cup white sugar
1/2 tsp. salt
1 tsp. cinnamon
1 tsp. ginger
1 tsp. nutmeg or allspice
1/8 tsp. cloves
2 eggs, slightly beaten

Blend pumpkin and milk together. Mix sugar and spices together and stir in pumpkin mixture. Add eggs. Mix well. Pour into 9-inch unbaked pie shell. Bake at 425 degrees for 15 minutes. Reduce heat to 350 and bake 45 minutes or until inserted knife comes out clean.

Pugsly's Pumpkin Pie

2 cups cooked pumpkin
3/4 cups sugar
2 tsp. cinnamon
1/2 tsp. nutmeg
1/4 tsp. ground cloves
3 eggs, slightly beaten
1 cup light cream
1 9-inch unbaked pie shell
1/2 tsp. salt

Combine pumpkin, spices, sugar and salt. Blend in eggs and cream. Pour into pie shell. Bake at 400 degrees about 45 minutes or until knife inserted in the center comes out clean.

Pecan Pumpkin Pie - sprinkle mixture over the pie for the last 10 minutes of baking:
2 Tbs. butter
1/4 cup brown sugar
1 Tbs. grated orange rind
3/4 cup whole pecans

Traditional Pie Crust

3 cups all-purpose flour
1 teaspoon salt
1 cup cold unsalted butter or 1 cup shortening or a half cup of each
5-9 tablespoons ice cold water

In a medium bowl, combine the flour and salt. Whisk to combine. Cut butter into small pieces. Work the fat into the flour using a fork. Don't overwork the dough. Add the ice water a small amount at a time, stirring after each addition.

The pie crust should just start to come together and should stick together when you press some in your hand. When the dough comes together, form it into a uniform mound and separate it into two pieces. Press each half into a ball.

Chill for 15-30 minutes. Then roll on a floured pastry board and use as directed in the pie recipe.

> **Fun Bat Fact:** What would Hallowe'en be without Jack-o-Lanterns or pumpkin pie? Without the help of bats, we might not have Mr. Lantern's spooky light or this yummy autumn dessert.

Graywing's Graham Cracker Pie Crust
1 1/4 cups finely-ground graham cracker crumbs (about 1 sleeve of crackers)
2 tablespoons sugar
5 tablespoons butter, melted
Preheat oven to 350 degrees.

Stir together graham cracker crumbs, sugar, and butter in a bowl until evenly combined. Press mixture evenly onto bottom and up the sides of a 9-inch (4-cup) pie plate. Use fingers, a spoon, or the back of a measuring cup to do this. Bake crust on the middle oven rack for 10 minutes, then remove and let cool.

To leave the crust unbaked, refrigerate for at least an hour before filling. The crust will be crumbly when you dish the pie and the flavor won't be as rich as if it were baked.

Chocolate Cookie Pie Crust:
16 plain chocolate cookies, crushed into very small pieces
3 tablespoons unsalted butter, melted

Preheat oven to 350 degrees.
Stir together chocolate cookie crumbs and butter in a bowl until evenly combined. Press mixture evenly onto bottom and up the sides of a 9-inch pie plate. Use fingers, a spoon, or the back of a measuring cup to do this. Bake crust on the middle oven shelf for 10 minutes, then remove and let cool.

To leave the crust unbaked, refrigerate for at least an hour before filling.

Chocolate Mousse Pie
Dark chocolate and espresso add the slightly bitter notes needed to balance this dessert. Remember, the higher the cacao percentage, the less sweet the chocolate.

3/4 cup chilled heavy cream, divided
4 large egg yolks
1/4 cup espresso or strong coffee, room temperature
1/8 teaspoon kosher salt
3 tablespoons sugar, divided
6 ounces semisweet chocolate (61-72% cacao), chopped
2 large egg whites
1 baked 9 inch pie shell - or omit the pie shell and scoop into dessert cups instead.

Beat 1/2 cup cream in a medium bowl until stiff peaks form; cover and chill. Combine egg yolks, espresso, salt, and 2 tablespoons sugar in a large metal bowl. Set over a saucepan of gently simmering water (do not allow bowl to touch water). Cook, whisking constantly, until mixture is lighter in color and almost doubled in volume and a candy thermometer inserted into the mixture registers 160°F, about 1 minute. Remove bowl from pan. Add chocolate; whisk until melted and smooth. Let stand, whisking occasionally, until room temperature. Beat egg whites in another medium bowl until foamy. Gradually beat in remaining 1 tablespoon sugar and beat until firm peaks form. Fold egg whites into chocolate in 2 additions; fold whipped cream into mixture just to blend.

Scoop mousse into pie shell or among six teacups. Chill until firm, at least 2 hours.
Mousse can be made 1 day ahead; cover and keep chilled. Let stand at room temperature for 10 minutes before serving.

Before serving, whisk remaining 1/4 cup cream in a small bowl until soft peaks form; dollop over mousse.

Fruity's No Bake Blueberry Cream Cheese Pie

4 ounces cream cheese, softened
1/2 cup confectioners' sugar
1/2 cup heavy whipping cream, whipped
Pastry for single-crust pie (9 inches), baked*
2/3 cup sugar 1/4 cup cornstarch
1/2 cup water
1/4 cup lemon juice
3 cups fresh or frozen blueberries

In a small bowl, beat cream cheese and confectioners' sugar until smooth. Fold in whipped cream. Spread into pie shell. In a large saucepan, combine the sugar, cornstarch, water and lemon juice until smooth; stir in blueberries. Bring to a boil over medium heat; cook and stir for 2 minutes or until thick. Cool. Spread over cream cheese layer. Refrigerate until serving.

Fresh Blueberry Pie

3/4 cup sugar
3 tablespoons cornstarch
1/8 teaspoon salt
1/4 cup cold water
5 cups fresh blueberries, divided
1 tablespoon butter
1 tablespoon lemon juice
1 refrigerated pie crust (9 inches), baked*

In a saucepan over medium heat, combine sugar, cornstarch, salt and water until smooth. Add 3 cups blueberries. Bring to a boil; cook and stir for 2 minutes or until thickened and bubbly. Remove from heat. Add butter, lemon juice and remaining berries; stir until butter is melted. Cool. Pour into pastry shell. Refrigerate until serving.

Fresh Strawberry pie

1 pie crust (9 inches)*
3/4 cup sugar
2 tablespoons cornstarch
1 cup water
1 package (3 ounces) strawberry gelatin
4 cups sliced fresh strawberries
Fresh mint, optional
Whipped cream, optional

In a small saucepan, combine the sugar, cornstarch and water until smooth. Bring to a boil; cook and stir for 2 minutes or until thickened. Remove from the heat; stir in gelatin until dissolved. Refrigerate for 15-20 minutes or until slightly cooled. Meanwhile, arrange strawberries in the crust. Pour gelatin mixture over berries. Refrigerate until set. Garnish with mint if desired.

*Pie crust recipes on the next page.

Ariel's Almond Flour Pie Crust

1 1/2 cups blanched almond flour
1/4 cup + 2 Tablespoons coconut flour
Pinch salt
1 egg white
2 Tablespoons cold almond milk or water
1/4 cup cold butter

In the bowl of a food processor, pulse the almond flour, coconut flour and salt a few times to break up all of the clumps. In a small bowl, whisk together the egg white and almond milk or water. Add the butter and pulse until it is broken into clumps slightly smaller than a pea. With the processor running, add the egg/water mixture in a thin stream until the dough forms a ball.

Turn off the machine and let it sit for 15 seconds before proceeding to allow the flour to absorb the moisture from the liquid. Turn the dough out on to a piece of wax or parchment paper, gather into a ball and press into a thick disc. Cover with another piece of wax or parchment paper and roll into a flat disc about 10"-11" in diameter.

Loosen the parchment from both sides of the dough and then carefully slide the dough into a lightly greased 9" pie or tart pan. Or simply turn the dough directly into a greased pie pan and use the heel of your hand to gently spread the dough. Refrigerate for at least 30 minutes before using.

To pre-bake: Preheat the oven to 350F. Once preheated, transfer the pan from the fridge to the oven without letting it warm to room temperature and bake for 10 minutes until the edges begin to turn slightly golden. Remove from oven and cool slightly before filling and finishing the baking process. **(Note: If the recipe does not call for pre-baking the pie shell, skip this step).**

Whole Wheat Pie Crust

3 cups white whole wheat or whole wheat pastry flour
1 teaspoon salt
1/2 teaspoon baking soda
1 cup cold unsalted butter, cut into smaller pieces
3 tablespoons orange juice
1/3 cup buttermilk
2-6 tablespoons ice cold water

In a medium bowl, combine the flour, salt, and baking soda. Whisk to combine.

Work the butter into the flour using a fork. Add the orange juice and buttermilk and stir to combine. Add the ice water a small amount at a time, stirring after each addition. This pie crust should just form a ball when you stir it. Don't make it too dry; whole wheat flour absorbs more liquid than white flour. When the dough comes together, form it into a uniform mound. Separate the dough into two pieces. Press each half into a round disc and chill for 15-20 minutes. Then roll and use as directed in the recipe.

Traditional pie crust recipe on page six.

Dusky's Crustless Zucchini, Corn and Tomato Quiche with Feta

2 cups zucchini, cut in 1/3-inch thick cubes
2 cups yellow squash, cut in 1/3-inch thick cubes
coarse salt
1 tablespoon olive oil
1 cup shallots, thinly sliced
1/3 cup red bell peppers, thinly sliced in short strips
3 cloves garlic, minced
fresh cracked black pepper
1 cup fresh organic corn on the cob
2/3 cup Roma tomatoes, diced, seeds and ribs removed
1 heaping tablespoon fresh parsley, chopped
1 heaping tablespoon fresh basil, chopped
1 heaping tablespoon fresh chives, chopped
1 teaspoon dill, fresh or dried (not ground)
1 cup crumbled feta cheese
butter, for greasing pan
3 eggs
3/4 cup heavy cream
3/4 cup whole milk
2 tablespoons grated parmesan

2-6 hours ahead of time toss the zucchini and yellow squash together in a large colander set over a bowl with 1/2 teaspoon coarse salt or 1/4 teaspoon table salt to drain excess water. Cover and refrigerate 2-6 hours.

Heat oil in a large frying pan over medium-low heat and saute shallots, peppers and garlic 5 minutes, stirring often. Season lightly with salt and pepper. Turn off heat and add squash, corn, tomatoes, all the herbs and the feta. Toss well. Taste and season with salt and pepper if needed.

Preheat oven to 400 degrees. Butter an 11x8 casserole dish or a deep dish pie pan. In a large bowl beat eggs, whisk in heavy cream and whole milk until well combined. Add the veggie mixture to the prepared dish and spread out evenly. Pour the milk mixture slowly over the entire top. Sprinkle with parmesan cheese.

Bake 35 - 40 minutes until the center is set. Serve hot or at room temperature.

Be creative! Use dfferent veggies and cheeses! For example, for a more Mediterranean twist, eggplant and mozzarella instead of squash, onions instead of shallots, and oregano instead of dill, and eliminate the corn.

Fun Bat Fact: Bats play a significant role in combating corn crop pests, saving more than 1 billion a year in crop damages around the world (National Academy of Sciences).

Maureen H's Mushroom Parmesan (recipe is batty - you have to wing it and play it by ear)

Make the sauce ahead of time.

6 or 8 large Portobello mushrooms
1 cup Panko or homemade bread crumbs; seasoned with salt, pepper and garlic powder

Butter
Olive oil
2 gloves fresh garlic, chopped or crushed
One medium onion
One large bell pepper
Fresh basil
Fresh parsley chopped
One carton Pomi brand chopped tomatoes (26 oz.) and one carton Pomi tomato puree (26 oz.)
Parmesan cheese
Mozzarella cheese
Red wine

Clean mushrooms, carefully remove the stems. Chop the stems finely and saute' them in butter until tender. Stir in breadcrumbs. Add wine. Mixture should be moist but not wet. Stuff the mushrooms with the mixture.

Sauce: In a large sauce pan, saute' garlic and onion in olive oil on medium heat until onion is tender. (Be careful not to burn the garlic). Add the pepper and cook until tender. Add the Pomi products and slowly bring to a boil. Reduce heat and simmer. Add the parsley and basil leaves and simmer for at least an hour. Of course you can use sauce you've made from your own garden tomatoes instead. Place stuffed mushrooms in a large baking dish with a little wine, water and butter on the bottom. Sprinkle with grated Parmesan cheese and top each one generously with sauce. Slice or shred the mozzarella and place it on top. Bake in a 350 degree oven until cheese on top starts to brown.

Cos' Stuffed Zucchini Boats
1/2 white onion
2 cloves garlic, minced
2 teaspoons cinnamon
1 teaspoon oregano
Pinch of salt and pepper
Diced tomatoes, excess juices drained (2 cups)
Feta cheese, cut into chunks
1 cup cooked brown rice
1 large zucchini, halved

Preheat the oven to 350 degrees F. As the oven heats, mix the onion, garlic, cinnamon, oregano, salt and pepper together. Place it in a skillet over medium heat and cook. Add the rice. Set aside. Halve the zucchini and scoop out the seeds, creating a trough in each one. Top with chunks of feta and place the boats on a baking sheet. Bake for 43-45 minutes.

Murciélago's Garden Fresh Salsa

4-5 cup diced tomatoes, any variety (about 5-6 med/lg tomatoes)
1 cup diced onion (red or white)
1 green bell pepper chopped
1 chili pepper roasted and chopped
1/2 cup sliced green onions
1 1/2 Tbsp. minced garlic
3/4 cup chopped cilantro (slice it up stems and all)
4 Tbsp fresh lime juice (about 2 limes)
1 tsp. kosher salt
1/8-1/4 tsp chipotle chili powder
optional: 1 jalapeno, seeded and diced
6 oz tomato juice

First, roast the chili peppers. Grill or broil them until completely blackened. Leave for 20-30 minutes. Peel off skin, deseed and chop.

While the peppers are cooking or steaming, combine tomatoes, onions, green onions, garlic, cilantro, lime juice and salt and chipotle powder, and the jalapeno. Stir to combine. Add tomato juice. Process in a food processor. Put the salsa in a container in the refrigerator and chill it for several hours before serving. Salsa has to "siesta" for a while to reach perfection.

Fresh Tomatillo Salsa

8-9 fresh tomatillos, husks removed, cleaned, and chopped
1 fresh jalapeno, deseeded, deveined, and chopped (more if you want spicier)
2 cloves garlic
1 handful fresh cilantro
1 medium onion, chopped
2 Tbsp fresh squeezed lime juice
1 - 2 tsp salt

Place all ingredients in food processor. Pulse until desired consistency is reached. Enjoy it right away or chill it for more flavor later.

Fresh Guacamole
1 avocado - peeled, pitted, and diced
1 Roma (plum) tomato, diced
small red onion, diced
1 chile pepper, seeded and minced
pinch or two kosher salt
pinch or two ground black pepper
juice from one clove garlic
3 drops hot sauce
6 cilantro leaves, minced
fresh lime juice

Combine the avocado, tomato, onion, chile, salt, pepper, garlic juice, hot sauce, and cilantro leaves in a bowl and mix. Pour lime juice over the top of the guacamole. Serve immediately. To store for later use, place avocado pit in a bowl with the guacamole, cover and store in refrigerator.

Echo's Hearty Veggie Stew

1 tablespoon vegetable oil
1 1⁄2 cups sliced onions
2 garlic cloves, minced
1 cup carrot, cut into 1-inch-thick slices
1 cup celery, cut into 1-inch-thick slices
4 cups mushrooms, cut into quarters
3 medium potatoes, unpeeled, cut into 1-inch chunks
Tomatoes, coarsely chopped - about 4-6 cups
2 cups cooked kidney beans
1 cup tomato sauce
1 cup water
1 teaspoon dried thyme
1 bay leaf
salt and pepper
3 tablespoons flour
1⁄4 cup water
1⁄4 cup red wine

Heat oil in a large, heavy saucepan over medium heat. Add onions, garlic, carrots, celery, and mushrooms. Cook 10 minutes, stirring frequently. Add small amounts of water, if necessary, to prevent sticking. Add remaining ingredients, except flour, 1/4 cup water, and wine. Cover, reduce heat to low, and simmer 30 minutes, or until vegetables are tender. Stir occasionally while cooking.

In a small bowl, gradually stir flour into 1/4 cup water until smooth. Add to stew, along with wine. Cook, stirring, 5 more minutes. Remove and discard bay leaf before serving.

Yummy Veggie Chili

1 tablespoon olive oil
1/2 medium onion, chopped
2 bay leaves
1 teaspoon ground cumin
2 tablespoons dried oregano
1 tablespoon salt
2 stalks celery, chopped
2 green bell peppers, chopped
2 jalapeno peppers, chopped
3 cloves garlic, chopped

2 green chili peppers, chopped
3 (28 ounce) cans whole peeled tomatoes, crushed
1/4 cup chili powder
1 tablespoon ground black pepper
1 (15 ounce) can kidney beans, drained*
1 (15 ounce) can garbanzo beans, drained
1 (15 ounce) can black beans
1 (15 ounce) can whole kernel corn*

Heat the olive oil in a large pot over medium heat. Stir in the onion, and season with bay leaves, cumin, oregano, and salt. Cook and stir until onion is tender, then mix in the celery, peppers, garlic.

When vegetables are heated through, reduce heat to low, cover pot, and simmer 5 minutes. Mix the tomatoes into the pot. Season with chili powder and pepper. Stir in the kidney beans, garbanzo beans, and black beans. Bring to a boil, reduce heat to low, and simmer 45 minutes. Stir in the corn, and continue cooking 5 minutes before serving.

Top with grated cheddar cheese.

* To use dry beans instead, follow directions on the package. Use fresh or frozen corn instead and add a cup of water.

13

Foxy's Fruit Smoothies

Blueberry Fruit Smoothie
Serves: 1
  ½ cup frozen blueberries
  ¼ cup unsweetened cranberry juice
  1-2 bananas
Place all ingredients in a blender and blend until smooth.

Easy Peach Smoothie
serves 2
  5 ounces vanilla yogurt
  1½ cup fresh or frozen peaches
  ½ cup crushed ice
  ¾ cup coconut milk (or milk of choice)
  ¼ teaspoon ground cinnamon
  ½ teaspoon sugar
  Combine all ingredients in a blender until smooth.

Banana Smoothie
serves 2
  3 ripe bananas, peeled
  11/2 cups unsweetened almond milk
  1 tablespoon honey
  1 cup crushed or cubed ice
Place all ingredients in a blender and process 1 to 2 minutes or until smooth. Serve immediately.

Fruity Tangy Smoothie
  1 kiwi, sliced
  1 banana, peeled and chopped
  1 cup blueberries
  1 cup sliced strawberries
  1/2 cup orange juice
  1 (8 ounce) container peach yogurt.
  In a blender, blend the kiwi, banana, blueberries, strawberries, ice, orange juice, and yogurt until smooth.

Simple Spinach Fruit Smoothie
  1 cup almond milk or fruit juice
  1 tablespoon honey if using almond milk
  1/2 cup plain yogurt if using juice
  1 banana
  1 large handful spinach
  1 cup frozen strawberries blueberries, pineapple, or mango
  Place ingredients into blender in order listed. Blend until smooth and serve!

Orange Julius
  1 cup milk whole, 2%, or skim
  2 teaspoons vanilla extract
  1 6- ounce orange juice concentrate
  1/2 cup sugar
  1 1/2 cups ice
  Add ingredients to a blender and blend on high until smooth.

Zurie's Double Chocolate Zucchini Muffins

4 cups flour
1 1/2 cup sugar
1/2 cup cocoa
1 tsp baking soda
1/2 tsp baking powder
 3/4 tsp salt
1 tsp cinnamon
1 1/2 cup oil
1 1/2 cup milk
3 eggs
2 tsp vanilla
2 cups shredded zucchini
1 1/2 cup semi sweet chocolate chips

Mix the wet ingredients together in a bowl with a whisk. Add the zucchini to the wet ingredients. Mix all of the dry ingredients in a separate bowl with a wooden spoon.

Pour the wet ingredients into the dry and stir, just until combined. Fold in the chocolate chips.

Line your muffin tin with cupcake holders and fill a bit more than 2/3 of the way full. Bake at 350 for 17 minutes.

Pip's Fresh Peach Coffee Cake

Streusel Ingredients
½ cup sugar
1 cup all-purpose flour
8 tablespoons butter, softened
1 teaspoon ground cinnamon
pinch of salt

Cake Ingredients
8 tablespoons butter, softened
1 cup sugar
2 large eggs, room temperature
1 cup whole milk plain yogurt, room temperature
1 teaspoon vanilla extract
2 cups all purpose flour
1 teaspoon ground cinnamon
pinch of ground nutmeg
1 teaspoon baking powder
½ teaspoon baking soda
½ teaspoon salt
2½ cups fresh, ripe but firm, peaches, peeled and diced (about 3 medium peaches)

Preheat oven to 350 degrees. Lightly grease two 8-inch round pans, or one 9x13 pan.

Prepare streusel: In a medium bowl, whisk together the sugar, flour, cinnamon, and pinch of salt.
With your hands, work the softened butter into the flour mixture until resembles a coarse crumble.

Prepare Cake: In a medium bowl, cream together the butter and sugar until fluffy. Add eggs, being careful to beat after the addition of each egg. Beat in yogurt and vanilla.

In a separate bowl, sift together the flour, baking powder, baking soda, salt, and spices. Stir flour mixture into the wet batter until just combined - be careful not to over mix. Gently fold the peaches into the batter.

Pour into prepared pan(s) and spread evenly.

Top with streusel until batter is completely covered.

Bake for approximately 30 minutes, or until toothpick inserted in the center comes out clean.

Cool for at least 15 minutes before cutting and serving.

Karen V's Date Squares

1/2 lb. dates
2 cups oatmeal
1 1/3 cup brown sugar
1 cup flour
3/4 cup shortening (butter, veg. shortening)
1/2 tsp. salt
1/2 tsp. baking soda
1/2 cup water

Cook dates, water and 1/2 cup brown sugar and bring to a boil. Mix oatmeal, the rest of the brown sugar, flour, salt, and baking soda in a bowl. Put 1/2 of the oatmeal mixture in an 8 inch pan. Pat it into the pan. Add the cooked dates and spread them evenly on top. Put the rest of the oatmeal mixture on top of that. Bake at 375 degrees for 15 or 20 minutes, or until light brown.

Elvira's Fig-Date Bread

1 cup chopped pitted dates
1 cup chopped dried figs
4 Tbs. (1/2 stick) unsalted butter, at room temperature
1 1/2 tsp. baking soda
1 cup boiling water
1/2 cup sugar
1/2 cup chopped walnuts
2 eggs
3/4 cup all-purpose flour
3/4 cup whole wheat flour
1/2 tsp. baking powder
1/2 tsp. salt

Preheat oven to 350ºF. Grease and flour a 1-lb. loaf pan. In a large bowl, combine the dates, figs, butter and baking soda. Pour in the boiling water, stir well and let stand for 15 minutes. Using a whisk, beat the sugar, walnuts and eggs into the date mixture; set aside. In another bowl, stir together the all-purpose and whole wheat flours, baking powder and salt. Add to the date mixture and whisk until just blended. Spoon the batter into the prepared pan and bake until a toothpick inserted into the center of the loaf comes out clean, 50 to 60 minutes. Transfer the pan to a wire rack and let cool for 15 minutes, then turn the loaf out onto the rack and let cool completely. Makes 1 loaf.

Barny's Butternut Squash/Apple Soup

1 large butternut squash
1 Tbsp. extra-virgin olive oil
1 large red apple (skin on) sliced
sea salt and freshly ground pepper to taste
1 cup whole milk
1 Tbsp. finely chopped fresh basil

1/4 cup whiskey (optional)

Preheat the oven to 400 degrees. Prepare two large rimmed baking sheets with parchment paper. Slice the butternut squash in half lengthwise. Scoop out seeds and save them for roasting. Lay the butternut squash face up on one of the prepared baking sheets. Drizzle with the olive oil and use your hands to coat both halves of the squash. Sprinkle with sea salt and pepper. Roast for 50-55 minutes or until the squash is fork tender. Toss the seeds in oil, salt and/or spices of your choice and roast them at the same time.

Place the apples on the other rimmed baking sheet cut side up and roast for 25 minutes or until tender. Remove the squash and apples from the oven and set aside for 5 minutes to cool. Then use a spoon to remove the squash 'flesh' and transfer it to a food processor with the roasted apples and milk. Puree until smooth; season to taste with sea salt and pepper. Add more milk if you'd like a thinner soup consistency. Garnish with the seeds.

For a thicker soup, use 1/2 cup light cream or sour cream and 1/2 cup milk.

Pipistrillo's Italian Minestrone Soup

2 diced large carrots
1 large onion chopped
2 stalks celery thinly sliced
2 diced medium potatoes
1 teaspoon salt
1 teaspoon pepper
¼ cup butter
¼ cup olive oil
3 cups vegetable broth or stock
1 (19 ounce) can diced tomatoes and juice
1 leek trimmed, washed and thinly sliced
1 (14 ounce) can white kidney beans drained & rinsed
1 zucchini peeled & diced
1 (14 ounce) can red kidney beans drained & rinsed
parmesan cheese

Heat butter and oil in a large heavy pot over medium heat. Add ingredients and saute for about 10 minutes, stirring occasionally. Add broth, seasonings, tomatoes and zucchini simmering on low heat, stirring occasionally up to 30-35 minutes. Add the beans and simmer for another 15 minutes. Garnish each serving with a shaving of fresh parmesan.

For a heartier soup, while adding the beans add dried pasta as well.

Eptie's Easy Baked Risotto with Roasted Butternut Squash

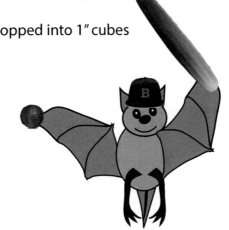

1 medium butternut squash, peeled and chopped into 1" cubes
3 tablespoons olive oil, divided
3-5 tablespoons fresh sage, chopped
Dash of salt
2 shallots, diced
1 stalk celery, diced
1 cup Arborio rice
3 1/2 cups vegetable broth
Salt and pepper to taste
More sage for garnishing (optional)

Heat the oven to 400 F. Toss the squash with 2 tablespoons olive oil, sage, and salt. Bake on a baking sheet for 20-25 minutes or until roasted, tossing once or twice. When the squash is nearly done, begin the risotto. In an oven-proof pot, heat 1 tablespoon oil over medium-high heat. Add the shallots and celery and cook until soft: 5-8 minutes. Add the rice and broth and bring to a boil.

Meanwhile, remove the squash from oven and raise the temperature to 425 F. Once the risotto comes to a boil, cover the pot and transfer it to the oven. Cook until the rice is tender and creamy, 20-25 minutes. Remove from the oven and stir in the squash. Add salt and pepper and garnish with sage if desired. Serve immediately.

Vesper's Vegetarian Reuben Sandwiches

2 cups sauerkraut, drained well
2 ounces sliced cheese (Swiss-style or jack cheese)
1/2 package Tofurky smoky maple bacon strips (or similar)
4 slices rye bread
Dressing
2 teaspoons mayo
2 teaspoons ketchup
1 teaspoon dill pickle relish
Dash or two of garlic powder
1/2 teaspoon Dijon mustard
Dash of pepper

Place the drained sauerkraut on 2 slices of bread, and top with slices of the cheese. Cut the breakfast strips in half and lightly sauté them over medium heat. Place these on top of the cheese slices.

Combine the dressing ingredients and mix well. Then, spread the dressing on the remaining bread slices, and on top of the sandwiches.

Cook the assembled sandwiches on a grill, or fry them in a lightly oiled, non-stick pan over medium-high heat, until the bread is lightly browned and the cheese begins to melt. Serve the sandwiches with kosher dill pickles, cole slaw, chips, or all three!

Chiro's Corn and Veggie Enchiladas Serves 6 (12 enchiladas total)

Corn sauce
2 cloves garlic, un-peeled
2 10-ounce packages frozen corn
1 cup soy milk
1/8 teaspoon cayenne pepper
Salt and freshly ground pepper, to taste

Enchilada ingredients
1 teaspoon Canola oil
8 ounces button mushrooms, wiped clean, stemmed, and sliced
10 ounces fresh spinach, stemmed and chopped
1 small onion, chopped
1/2 teaspoon salt
Freshly ground pepper, to taste
12 corn tortillas
1 cup shredded cheddar cheese
Tomato salsa

To prepare the corn sauce: 1. Roast the un-peeled garlic cloves in a large, heavy skillet over medium-high heat, shaking the pan often, until lightly browned, about 8 minutes. Add half the corn and cook, stirring often, until lightly toasted, about 8 minutes. **2.** Reserve the garlic, and transfer the corn from the skillet to a blender. Peel the garlic and add it to the blender of toasted corn, along with the soy milk and cayenne. Blend until smooth. Strain through a sieve into a bowl. **3.** Toast the remaining corn in the skillet. Stir the toasted corn into the corn sauce, season withsalt and pepper, and set aside.

To prepare the enchiladas: 1. Preheat the oven to 350 F. Coat a 9-by-13-inch pan with shortening. **2.** Heat the oil in a large, non-stick skillet over medium-high heat. Add the mushrooms and cook, stirring often, until softened (about 4 minutes). Add the spinach and cook until it's just wilted (about 2 minutes). Drain off excess liquid. Remove from heat and stir in the onion, salt, and pepper. **3.** Toast the tortillas by placing them directly on a burner (gas or electric) set at medium heat. Turn each tortilla frequently with tongs, until golden (30 to 60 seconds). **4.** Sprinkle a generous tablespoon of the cheddar cheese shreds down the center of a tortilla. Cover the cheese with a scant 1/4 cup of the spinach mixture. **5.** Fold one side of the tortilla over the filling, then roll up tightly. Place the enchilada seam-side down in the prepared dish. Repeat with the remaining tortillas, cheese, and spinach mixture. Spoon the corn sauce over the enchiladas, covering them completely. **6.** Cover the baking dish with foil. Bake for 25 minutes, or until heated through. Uncover and bake for 5 minutes. **7.** Top with salsa and serve immediately.

Fun Bat Fact: Baby bats are called "pups." Most mother bats give birth to a single pup each year, but some have twins and others can have triplets, quadruplets and even quintuplets - the same as human moms!

Winghand's White Bean Pizza

Dough
3 cups flour
2 packets baker's yeast
2 tablespoons sugar
3 cloves crushed garlic
1/4 cup olive oil 1/4 cup melted margarine
1 cup warm water

Topping
1 tablespoon olive oil
3 garlic cloves, finely minced
One 15.5-ounce can of cannellini beans
1/4 teaspoon salt
1/4 teaspoon black pepper
1/2 cup water or vegetable stock
3 tablespoons fresh basil, chopped
2 medium ripe Roma tomatoes, cut into 1/4-inch slices

Make the crust
Mix the yeast and water together in a bowl and set aside for a few minutes. Add the other ingredients and mix well. Knead the dough, then set it in a greased bowl (covered) for about 30minutes. Punch down the dough and form the crust on on a baking sheet, cake pan, or pizza stone.

Make the toppings
In a large skillet, heat the oil over medium heat. Add the garlic and cook until softened (about 2 minutes). Add the beans, salt, and pepper. Mash the beans to break them up, then stir in the water and simmer, stirring occasionally, until the mixture is creamy (about 8 minutes). Stir in the basil and set aside. Spread the bean mixture evenly on top of the dough round, to within 1/2 inch of the edges. Arrange the tomato slices on top, and season with salt and pepper to taste. Bake at 400 F in a preheated oven until the crust is browned, 12 to 15 minutes.

Variation - veggie topping
2 cups tomatoes, roughly chopped
3 fresh basil leaves (or 1 teaspoon dried)
1 teaspoon dried oregano
2 tablespoons parmesan cheese (plus additional for topping)
1 cup jack cheese, thinly sliced
1 package mozzarella cheese

Preheat the oven to 450 F. Next, place the thinly sliced jackcheese across the bottom of the dough. Cover that with the shredded mozzarella. Spread it out so you don't see any of the pizza dough coming through. Place the chopped tomatoes into a food processor along with the basil, oregano, and parm. pulse for just a few seconds. Spread the tomato mixture over the cheese. Sprinkle with additional parmesan. Place the pizza in the preheated oven for 20 to 25 minutes. The dough should be showing a nice golden color.

Silvie's Sweet Potato Gnocchi "Pillows" with Sage Butter

2 large red-skinned sweet potatoes (about 2 pounds)
1 teaspoon sea salt
1/2 teaspoon ground nutmeg
1/4 teaspoon freshly ground black pepper
2-1/2 to 3-1/2 cups all-purpose flour, plus extra for rolling
1/2 cup margarine
1/2 cup fresh sage leaves

Preheat the oven to 425 degrees. Pierce the potatoes with a fork, place in a baking pan, and bake until fully cooked: 45 to 60 minutes. Remove from oven and let sit until cool enough to handle. Cut the potatoes in half lengthwise. Scoop the flesh out of each sweet potato into a medium bowl. Thoroughly mash the sweet potatoes while they are still warm, then cool.

Add salt, nutmeg, and pepper to the sweet potatoes. Add flour, 1/2 cup at a time, mixing well with a spoon to combine. Once a soft, slightly sticky dough has formed, divide it into six portions.

Flour the work surface and your hands. Roll each portion of dough into ropes about 1/2 inch in diameter. Each rope will be approximately 7 to 9 inches long. Dip a sharp knife in flour and cut each rope into 1-inch "pillows." If desired, roll each on fork tines to make decorative ridges.

Fill a medium saucepan with heavily salted water and bring it to a boil. **Heat the margarine and sage** until the margarine begins to bubble.

When the water is boiling, reduce the heat to a gentle simmer. drop in the gnocchi, about 20 at a time. The gnocchi will float to the surface in about 4 minutes.

Continue to cook about 30 seconds more. Using a slotted spoon, immediately transfer the gnocchi to the skillet of butter sauce. *Let cook,* turning frequently, for 1 to 2 minutes, until all the gnocchi are cooked. Serve immediately,

Maureen H's Stuffed Peppers with Mushrooms

2 large green peppers
8 oz. mushrooms, sliced
1/4 cup chopped onion
2 cups tomato sauce, divided
1 cup cooked rice
1/8 teaspoon salt
1 clove garlic, minced
1/8 teaspoon pepper

Cut tops off peppers and remove seeds. Place peppers in a large saucepan and cover with water. Bring to a boil; cook for 3 minutes. Drain and immediately place in ice water; invert on paper towels.

In a small skillet, saute mushrooms, garlic and onion over medium heat until onions are soft. Be careful not to burn the garlic. Remove from the heat. Stir in 1 cup tomato sauce, rice, salt, garlic powder and pepper. Spoon into pepers.

Place in an ungreased shallow 2-qt. baking dish. Drizzle with remaining tomato sauce. Cover and bake at 350° for 25-30 minutes or until peppers are tender.

Mushroom and Brussels Sprout Hash

2 tablespoons olive oil
1 small shallot, minced
2 big handfuls mushrooms
1 clove garlic, minced
3 big handfuls Brussels sprouts
salt and pepper to taste
juice of half a lemon
1 tablespoon olive oil
2 large eggs

Wipe mushrooms with a moist paper towel to remove any excess dirt. Slice mushrooms into quarters. Set aside.

Rinse Brussels sprouts. Slice sprouts into ribbons by thinly slicing horizontally from top to bottom. Set aside.

In a medium skillet, heat olive oil over medium heat. Add shallots and cook until translucent and just browned, about 4 minutes. Add the mushrooms and a pinch of salt. Cook down until mushrooms are softened and beginning to brown. Add garlic and cook for one minute more. Add Brussels sprout ribbons and increase heat to med-high.

Toss to combine and cook until sprouts and mushrooms are softened and browned. Once browned and cooked well, remove from the heat, add lemon juice and toss again.

Connie W's Chocolate Bat Cookies

3⁄4 cup all-purpose flour, plus more
all-purpose flour, for dusting
1⁄4 cup unsweetened cocoa
3⁄4 teaspoon coarse salt
1⁄4 teaspoon baking powder
2 tablespoons unsalted butter, room temperature
1⁄4 cup granulated sugar
1⁄4 cup light brown sugar
1 large egg
1 large egg yolk
4 ounces semisweet chocolate, melted and cooled
1⁄2 teaspoon pure vanilla extract
1⁄4 cup chocolate frosting

Whisk together flour, cocoa, salt, and baking powder. Beat butter and sugars with a mixer on medium speed until pale and fluffy. Beat in egg, yolk, chocolate, and vanilla. Reduce speed to low. Add flour mixture, and beat until just combined. Shape into a disk, cover with wax paper, and refrigerate 1 hour.

On a lightly floured surface, roll out dough to 1/8 inch thick. Cut out 36 rounds with a 2-inch cutter, and space 1 inch apart on parchment-lined baking sheets. Using an aspic cutter set, cut a triangle, point side up, in the center of half the cookies, and then use a half-moon cutter to make one "wing" on each side of the triangle. Refrigerate 30 minutes.

Preheat oven to 375. Bake until set, 7 to 9 minutes. Let cool. Top each uncut cookie with 1 teaspoon frosting and a cutout cookie.

Chocolate Zucchini Muffins

3 eggs
2 cups white sugar
1 cup vegetable oil
1/3 cup unsweetened cocoa powder
1 1/2 teaspoons vanilla extract
2 cups grated zucchini
3 cups all-purpose flour
1 teaspoon baking soda
1/2 teaspoon baking powder
1 teaspoon salt
1/4 teaspoon ground cinnamon
1/4 teaspoon ground nutmeg
1/4 teaspoon ground cloves
1/4 teaspoon ground cardamom

Preheat oven to 350 degrees F. Lightly grease two 12 cup muffin tins. In a large bowl beat the eggs. Beat in the sugar and oil. Add the cocoa, vanilla, zucchini and stir well. Stir in the flour, baking soda, baking powder, salt, and spices. Mix until just moist. Pour batter into prepared muffin tins filling 2/3 of the way full. Bake for 20 to 25 minutes. Remove from pan and let cool on a wire rack.

Lucy's Gingerbread Cake Cookies
Makes about 4 dozen cookies

3 cups all-purpose flour
1 teaspoon baking soda
1 teaspoon ground cinnamon
1 teaspoon ground ginger
1/2 teaspoon ground allspice
1/2 teaspoon ground cloves
1/2 teaspoon salt
1/4 teaspoon ground black pepper
8 tablespoons (1 stick) unsalted butter, at room temperature
1/4 cup vegetable shortening, at room temperature
1/2 cup packed light brown sugar
2/3 cup unsulfured molasses
1 large egg
Any coarse sugar

In a medium bowl whisk together the flour, baking soda, cinnamon, ginger, allspice, cloves, salt, and black pepper, and set aside.

Cream the butter and shortening until smooth and well-combined. Add the brown sugar and beat until fluffy and pale. Beat in the molasses and egg. With a spoon, gradually mix in the flour mixture. Divide dough in half. Refrigerate until firm, about 3 hours, or up to 2 days.

Preheat oven to 325°F. Pour a little of the coarse sugar into a small, shallow bowl. Break off a small piece of dough and form into a ball about 3/4 inches in diameter, or scoop out dough with a small ice cream scoop. Dip the top in the sugar and place on a parchment-lined baking sheet. Repeat with remaining dough, spacing cookies about 1 inch apart. Bake for 10-12 minutes, or until edges of cookies are firm and look dry, rotating baking sheet halfway through baking.

Cool on the baking sheet for 2 minutes, then transfer to wire racks to cool completely. Store in an airtight container for up to 5 days.

Allie's Green Bean Casserole with Almonds

2 pounds Fresh Green Beans, Ends Cut Off
3 cloves Garlic, Minced
1/2 whole Large Onion, Chopped
4 Tablespoons Butter
4 Tablespoons All-purpose Flour
2-1/2 cups Whole Milk
1/2 cup Half-and-Half
1-1/2 teaspoon Salt, More To Taste
Freshly Ground Black Pepper, To Taste
1/8 teaspoon Cayenne Pepper
1 cup Grated Sharp Cheddar Cheese
1 jar (4 Ounce) Sliced Pimentoes, Drained
1 cup Panko Bread Crumbs
1 cup Slivered Almonds
Vegetable Broth If Needed For Thinning

Blanch the green beans: drop them into salted boiling water and cook for about 3 to 4 minutes. Remove them from the water with a slotted spoon and immediately plunge them into a bowl of ice cold water to stop the cooking process. Drain beans and set aside.

Over medium heat, saute' the diced onion and garlic and cook for 3 to 5 minutes, or until the onions are golden brown. Remove from heat and set aside.

In a separate skillet or saucepan, melt butter over medium heat. Sprinkle flour into the pan and whisk immediately to evenly mix it into the butter. Cook for a minute or two, then pour in milk and half and half. Continue cooking, whisking constantly, while sauce thickens, about 2 minutes. Add salt, pepper, and cayenne then add the grated cheddar. Stir while cheese melts. If sauce is too thick, splash in some broth as needed. Turn off heat.

Add pimentos to pan, then stir to combine. Pour over green beans and stir gently to combine. Pour into a baking dish and top with Panko crumbs and almonds.

Bake at 350 degrees for 30 minutes or until sauce is bubbly and Panko crumbs and almonds are golden.

Fun Bat Fact:
Bats eat moths and other insects that prey on nut producing plants, including walnuts, almonds, pecans, pistachios and cashews.

Cora P's Spiced Nuts

¾ cup sugar
1 tbsp. kosher salt
1 tbsp. chili powder
2 tsp cinnamon
2 tsp cayenne pepper
1 large egg white
2 cups unsalted cashews
2 cups unsalted almonds
Add peanuts or other nuts to make 4 cups if short on above

Preheat oven to 300 degrees. Coat a rimmed baking sheet with parchment and then cooking spray or oil. (just spray cookie sheet, but parchment makes easier cleanup). Whisk sugar and spices together. Beat egg white until frothy in a large bowl. Stir together until nuts are well coated. Spread in a single layer and bake for 40 – 45 minutes.

Let cool on baking sheet. You can make ahead and store at room temperature up to two days.

Chocolate Bark with Pistachios & Dried Cherries

¾ cup roasted, shelled pistachios, coarsely chopped
¾ cup dried cherries, or dried cranberries
1 teaspoon freshly grated orange zest
24 ounces bittersweet chocolate, finely chopped, divided

Line the bottom and sides of a jelly-roll pan or baking sheet with foil. (Take care to avoid wrinkles.) Toss pistachios with cherries (or cranberries) in a medium bowl. Divide the mix in half; stir orange zest into 1 half.

Melt 18 ounces chocolate in a double boiler over hot water. Stir often with a rubber spatula so it melts evenly. Remove the top pan and wipe dry. Stir in the remaining 6 ounces chocolate until thoroughly melted and smooth.

Add the pistachio mixture containing the orange zest to the chocolate; stir to mix well. Quickly scrape the chocolate on-to the prepared pan, spreading it to an even ¼ inch thick-ness with a rubber spatula. Sprinkle the remaining pistachio mixture on top; gently press it into the chocolate with your fingertips. Refrigerate, uncovered, just until set, about 20 minutes. **Invert the pan onto a large cutting board.** Remove the pan and peel off the foil. Using the tip of a sharp knife, score the chocolate lengthwise with 6 parallel lines. Break bark along the score lines. Break the strips of bark into 2- to 3-inch chunks.

The bark will keep in an airtight container in the refrigerator for up to 2 weeks.

Shadow's Savory Summer Cobbler

3 to 4 medium zucchini or summer squash cut into bite- size pieces
3 to 4 large tomatoes cut into bite size pieces
3 cloves garlic finely chopped
4 scallions finely chopped
1 lemon zested
1/4 fresh basil cut into ribbons (optional)

Topping

1 1/2 cups all-purpose or whole wheat flour
1/2 cup cornmeal
1 Tbsp baking powder
1/2 tsp salt
1 tsp black pepper
1 tsp smoked paprika
1/2 cup cheddar grated
1/2 cup butter
1 cup milk

Put the butter for the topping in the freezer for 30 minutes. Set the oven to 425 F.
Lightly oil any size baking dish that will accommodate the mixture and pile in the vegetables, garlic, scallions, lemon zest, and basil (if using). Pour the olive oil, salt, and pepper over top and mix it up with your   hands. Bake the vegetables for 25 minutes while you prepare the biscuit topping.

For the topping, measure out the flour, cornmeal, baking powder, salt, pepper, paprika and cheese into a bowl. Mix.

Once the butter is frozen, use a box grater to flake the butter into the flour mixture. Gently massage the butter into the flour with your fingers until it's crumbly but still clumpy. Add the milk and quickly bring the dough together. Don't knead the dough: lumpiness is fine and results in flaky topping. Put it in the fridge until the vegetables come out of the oven.

Once the vegetable mixture has cooked for 25 minutes, quickly top it with small clumps of biscuit dough. The vegetables should still be visible in some areas.

Bake for 10 to 25 minutes or until the vegetables are bubbly and the topping is lightly browned. Top with some more cheddar and some chopped herbs. Enjoy!

For a variation, swap the zucchini for eggplant. Chop the eggplant into bite-sized pieces, salt them, and set them aside for 30 minutes before continuing with the recipe as you would with the zucchini.

Sharon C's Pizza Stone Bread Recipe (makes two loaves)

1 envelope active dry yeast (2 1/4 teaspoons)
2 tablespoons lukewarm water
1 cup boiling water
3 tablespoons butter(1 tablespoon will be used
after baking)
1 teaspoon salt
1 tablespoon plus 1 teaspoon of sugar
3 cups flour
1 tablespoon corn meal *

Preheat oven 425°. On large pizza stone, sprinkle cornmeal in 2 areas-about 4" by 3" ovals in order to keep the bread from sticking to the stone. Place stone near stove to keep it warm.

In a small separate bowl, combine yeast and 1 teaspoon of sugar with lukewarm water. Let sit for at least 5 minutes until yeast is dissolved and starts to "proof."

In a large mixing bowl, pour boiling water over 2 tsp. of butter, salt and 1 tablespoon of sugar. Stir until smooth. Stir while adding 2 cups of the flour and the yeast. Then add remaining cup of flour. Stir until all combined. Dough will sticky, yet it should come free from spoon after stirring.

Place dough in the 2 separate areas on stone. Let rise in warm place for 10-40 minutes.

Bake in preheated oven for 18-20 minutes until golden brown. Once out of oven, use a metal spatula to loosen the bread from the stone. Butter the top of each loaf with remaining tablespoon of butter.

* Bats play a key role in the agricultural production of corn.

Andersen's Avocado Chocolate Pudding

1/4 cup butter or margarine
1 cup avocado puree
1 cup confectioners' sugar
1/2 cup unsweetened cocoa powder
1 tsp. pure vanilla extract
1/4 cup cornstarch

In a medium saucepan, melt the butter/margarine over low heat. Stir in the avocado puree, sugar, cocoa powder, and vanilla. Cook, mashing well with a rubber spatula to smooth out any lumps of avocado, until the mixture thickens (3-4 minutes). Remove from heat and gradually stir in the cornstarch. Serve warm.

Ricardo's Rum Sugar Plums

2 cups dried fruit
3 tablespoons Bacardi rum

Batter
1/4 cup (4 tablespoons) butter
1/2 cup brown sugar
1/4 teaspoon salt
1/4 teaspoon cinnamon
1/8 teaspoon ground allspice or 1/4 tsp ground ginger
1/8 teaspoon nutmeg
1/4 teaspoon baking powder
1 large egg
3/4 cup unbleached all-purpose flour
2 tablespoons boiled cider, or light or dark corn syrup
2 tablespoons light or dark corn syrup
1/2 cup chopped toasted pecans or walnuts
1/3 cup confectioner's sugar

Finely chop the fruit in a food processor. Combine with the liquor, cover, and let rest overnight. Or microwave the fruit and liquor (in a covered bowl) for about 1 minute, until the liquid is very hot. Leave the fruit covered and let cool to room temperature.

Preheat the oven to 350°F. Lightly grease two baking sheets. Combine the butter, sugar, salt, spices, and baking powder, then beat in the egg, scraping the bowl. Add the flour, then the cider, syrup, fruit (with remaining liquid), and nuts.

Drop the dough by teaspoonfuls onto the prepared baking sheets. Bake for 12 minutes; the cookies will look soft, and will just be starting to brown on the bottom. Remove the cookies from the oven, and let them cool. While the cookies are cooling, place the confectioner's sugar in a wax paper bag. While the cookies are still hot, gently squeeze them into balls. Place cookies in the bag, 6 or 8 at a time, and shake gently until they're coated with sugar.

Place on a rack to cool. Store airtight for several weeks.

Tips from the fruit bats: Use just one favorite dried fruit, or a combination such as cranberries, apricots, pineapple, and a bit of ginger. Or after squeezing them into balls, roll them in a shallow pan of flavored syrup to coat; you'll need about 1/3 cup of syrup. Try vanilla, pomegranate, white ginger, black currant. Place the cookies on a rack to dry. When they're still tacky but not wet, coat in sugar as directed above, and wrap well to store.

Aggie's Margaritas from Scratch (makes two)

3 oz tequila
2 oz Cointreau
1 1/2 oz fresh lime juice: Key limes are preferred
1/2 oz agave
1/2 oz fresh lemon juice
1/2 oz fresh orange juice
Lime slices for serving
Ice

Strain the margaritas evenly into two glasses before adding ice.

The next time you sip a margarita or a tequila sunrise, reflect on the contribution made to the tequila industry by long-nosed bats. These bats are the main pollinators of Century Plants (Agave) (Bat Conservation International).

Desmond's Classic Bloody Mary

1 lemon wedge
1 lime wedge
2 ounces vodka (Premium)
4 ounces tomato juice
2 dashes Tabasco Pepper Sauce
2 teaspoons prepared horseradish
2 dashes worcestershire
1 pinch celery salt
1 pinch ground black pepper
1 pinch smoked paprika

Combine all ingredients in a tall glass and stir well. Garnish with olives or celery leaves - or whatever strikes your fancy.

Gimly's Rum Gimlet

2 oz light Bacardi rum
1/2 oz lime juice
1 lime wedge

Pour the rum and lime juice into a mixing glass half filled with ice cubes. Stir well and strain into a cocktail glass. Garnish with a lime wedge and serve.

Durante's Tequila Sunrise

1 (1.5 fluid ounce) shot-glass tequila
3/4 cup freshly squeezed orange juice
Orange Juice, No Pulp, 59 oz
1/2 (1.5 fluid ounce) shot-glass grenadine syrup
1 slice orange for garnish
1 maraschino cherry for garnish

Stir or shake together tequila and orange juice. Fill a chilled 12 ounce glass with ice cubes; pour in orange juice mixture. Slowly pour in the grenadine, and allow it to settle to the bottom of the glass. Garnish with orange slice and cherry.

The Bacardi Family supports
Bat Conservation International

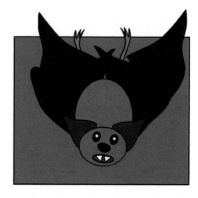

Vampire bats *don't* drink Bloody Marys.
Vampire bat moms *do* adopt orphaned pups.
Vampire bat moms *do* help each other while raising pups.

Quigly's Paleo Bread

1 1/2 cups almond flour
2 tablespoons coconut flour
1/4 cup flaxseed meal
1/4 teaspoon salt
1 1/2 teaspoons baking soda
5 medium chicken eggs (3 duck eggs)
1/4 cup oil
1 tablespoon agave (or honey)
1 tablespoon apple cider vinegar

Place almond flour, coconut flour, flax, salt and baking soda in a food processor and pulse the ingredients together. Add in eggs, oil, agve and vinegar and pulse. Pour batter into a greased 7.5 x 3.5" non-stick loaf pan. Bake at 350° F for about 40 minutes. Cool and serve.

Kittie's Kito Bread

1 cup almond flour
¾ cup arrowroot flour
½ cup golden milled flaxseed meal
1/3 cup coconut oil or butter
4 medium chicken eggs (2 duck eggs)
1/2 cup water room temp
1 teaspoon apple cider vinegar
½ teaspoon salt
2 teaspoons baking powder

Preheat oven to 350F. Line a standard bread pan with parchment paper. Combine all of the ingredients for the bread. Pour the batter into the loaf pan. Bake on 350F for 35 minutes until golden on top.

Note: batters can be easily mixed by hand. For variety, sprinkle with sesame seeds before baking or add ground sage and cheddar cheese to the batter.

Fun Bat Fact: Bats have lived on Earth for 50 million years!

Paleo Zucchini Fritters (Wheat Free)

2 zucchini, shredded (about 5 cups)
1 tsp salt
1/4 cup coconut flour
1 egg beaten
1 tsp black pepper
1/4 tsp cayenne pepper optional
Coconut oil or ghee for cooking

Shred the zucchini using a cheese grater or a food processor fitted with a shredding blade. Put the shredded zucchini in a large bowl. Sprinkle with the salt and toss well. After 10 minutes, rinse thoroughly under cold water. Squeeze all the moisture out of the zucchini until dry. Place in a different bowl. Add the coconut flour, egg and pepper. Stir to combine.

Heat a large skillet over medium-low heat. Melt a large spoonful of ghee or coconut oil in the pan. Pack a ¼ cup measuring cup with the zucchini mixture, pressing it down inside the cup. Turn the cup out onto the pan and flatten the zucchini into a patty: about 4 or 5 in a large skillet at one time.

Cook each side for 3 to 5 minutes or until nicely browned. Repeat until all the zucchini mixture is used up. Be sure to add more ghee or coconut oil to the pan each time a new batch is started.

Paleo Fruit and Nut Balls (Wheat Free)

2 cups walnuts, or other nut/seed of choice
1 cup shredded unsweetened coconut
2 cups soft dates, pitted
2 tbsps coconut oil
1/2 tsp salt
1 tsp vanilla extract

In a large food processor process the walnuts and coconut until crumbly. Add in the dates, coconut oil, vanilla and salt and process again until a sticky, uniform batter is formed.

Scoop the dough by heaping tablespoons, then roll to form balls. Arrange them on a baking sheet lined with parchment paper, then place in the freezer to set for at least an hour before serving.

Store the balls in a sealed container in the fridge for up to a week, or in the freezer for an even longer shelf life. Substitution Notes: use any other combination of nuts and dried fruits. The combinations are endless!

Cindy's Savory Peanut Rice w/ Mixed Veggies

2 cups Rice - cooked and cooled
1 tbsp Peanuts
1 cup Mixed Vegetables - (can be pre-cooked)
1 Onion - small, finely chopped
2 Chilies Green - slit (optional)
1 tsp Chana dal Beans
1 tsp Urad dal Lentils
1 tsp Mustard seeds
1 tsp Cumin seeds
¼ tsp Turmeric
8 - 10 Curry leaves to taste
Salt

For the Peanut-Sesame powder:
3 tbsp Dry Roasted Peanuts
1 tbsp Sesame seeds
2 Red Chili Dried (add more for spicier recipe)
2 - 3 cloves Garlic

Make the Peanut-Sesame spice powder: Dry roast peanuts, sesame seeds, dry red chilies and garlic cloves until golden. Cool slightly and grind to a coarse powder.

Heat 1tbsp oil in a pan, add chana dal, urad dal, peanuts, mustard seeds, cumin seeds and curry leaves; once the seeds start to splutter and dals turn golden, add the onions and fry till they turn translucent.

Next add green chilies and the mixed vegetables. Mix well, cover and cook till the veggies are tender.

Once the veggies are tender, add turmeric and the peanut spice powder, mix well. Add cooked rice and mix until well combined. Serve hot!!!

Plain Rice -Serves 2
2 cups water
1 cup white rice (plain, basmati or jasmine)
Pinch or two of salt

In a pot, combine the water, salt and uncooked rice. With the lid off, bring to a low boil over medium heat. Turn down the heat to low and put the lid on, leaving a gap so the steam can escape. Add rice and cook for about 20 minutes until the water is all gone and rice is fluffy.

Brown Rice
1 cup rice
2 ½ cups water

Place lid on pot and bring to a boil slowly. Turn down the heat and simmer the rice until all the water is absorbed.

L.B.'s Black Beans & Rice

1 lb dried black beans
3 cups vegetable broth
1 Tbs cumin
2 tsp chili powder
1/4 tsp saffron (optional)
2 garlic cloves, minced
1/4 onion, diced
1 tsp salt
1 cup brown rice, uncooked
12 cups water
1 lime, cut into wedges

Start by soaking the beans overnight or for at least 8 hours. Drain and rinse the beans and add them to a slow cooker. Add the cumin, chili powder, saffron, garlic cloves, onion. Pour in the vegetable broth. Cook on low for 8 hours or until beans are tender.

Once the beans are ready, make the rice. Pour the 12 cups of water in a large stock pot. Add the rice and bring to a boil. Allow to boil uncovered for 30 minutes. Drain the rice in a colander.

Return the rice to the stock pot, cover, and allow to steam for 10 minutes. Add 1 1/2 to 2 cups of beans to the rice. Stir to combine. Serve rice and beans with lime wedge(s.)

Bats, Beans and Rice (not a recipe)

Bats eat the insects that eat beans. They also provide a pest-control service in rice paddies - free of charge!

Basic Hummus

2 cups cooked chickpeas
1 Tbsp Tahini
1 Tbsp lemon juice
1 clove garlic, finely chopped
1 Tbsp olive oil
salt and pepper to taste

Mash the chickpeas, Tahini, lemon juice and garlic, olive oil, salt and pepper in a bowl. Slowly add 1/4 cup water until the mixture is smooth, creamy and light. Add more oil and Tahini for richer hummus. For smoother, lighter hummus, add more water.

If using a food processor, add all ingredients to the processor along with 1/8 cup water.

For variety, add more lemon juice, sesame oil instead of olive oil, roasted garlic or red pepper. Almost anything goes!

Tomasina's Tomato Pound Cake

Unsalted butter, for greasing pan
1½ cups all-purpose flour, plus more for dusting the pan
12 to 16 ounces of fresh tomatoes
2 teaspoons kosher salt, divided, plus more for sprinkling
1 cup finely grated Parmesan cheese
7 tablespoons unsalted butter
½ cup extra-virgin olive oil, plus more for brushing
4 large eggs
2 teaspoons baking powder
1 teaspoon freshly ground black pepper, plus more

Heat the oven to 350 degrees F. Butter and flour a 10-inch metal spring-form pan, cake pan, or pie pan.

Remove the cores and seeds from the tomatoes, slice then coarsely chop them. Place them in a colander set over a bowl, and toss with a teaspoon of salt. Let stand and drain: make the batter.

In a medium bowl, whisk together the 1 1/2 cups of flour, the remaining teaspoon of salt, the baking powder, and pepper until evenly combined.

Cream the Parmesan and butter until pale white and very fluffy. Add the eggs, and beat until smooth. Add the dry ingredients and mix until just combined. The mixture should be airy and light, with a mousse-like texture.

Spoon about half the batter into the prepared pan. Give the tomatoes a shake in the colander, then sprinkle half over the batter in the pan. Spoon the remaining batter into the pan, spread evenly, then sprinkle the rest of the tomatoes on top, lightly pressing them down into the batter. Brush the exposed tomatoes with more olive oil and, if desired, sprinkle on a little more salt and pepper.

Bake until the top is pale gold and a small knife inserted into the center of the cake comes out clean, about 40 to 45 minutes. Let the cake cool for 20 minutes before removing from the pan. Cool to room temperature before serving.

Fun Bat Fact: The millions of Mexican free-tailed bats at BCI's Bracken Cave in Central Texas eat tons of insects each summer night. And a favorite target in the United States and Mexico is an especially damaging pest called the corn earworm moth that attacks a host of commercial plants from artichokes to watermelons, and including tomatoes corn and cotton. It is estimated that free-tailed bats save cotton farmers in south-central Texas 3.7 billion dollars a year in crop damage and pesticide use, and of course that means fewer pesticides enter the ecosystem (BCI).

Basil's Heirloom Tomato Salad

4 medium heirloom tomatoes – cut in 1/4 slices
1 cup mixed heirloom cherry tomatoes
1lb fresh mozzarella, sliced
extra virgin olive oil
balsamic vinegar
sea salt to taste
freshly ground black pepper to taste
1/2 cup small basil leaves

Arrange the tomatoes and mozzarella on a large serving plate. Drizzle lavishly with olive oil and balsamic vinegar. Sprinkle with salt and pepper. Garnish with the basil and serve with sourdough or Italian country bread.

Artichoke Olive and Roasted Pepper Antipasto

3 red bell peppers - roasted
3 yellow bell peppers -roasted
2 garlic cloves
2 cans whole artichoke hearts
2/3 cup packed fresh flat-leaf parsley leaves
1 tbsp. extra-virgin olive oil
1 tbsp. unsalted butter
2 tbsp. fresh lemon juice
2/3 cups brine-cured black olives

Roast and peel peppers. Cut peppers into 3/4 inch wide strips. Mince garlic. Rinse and drain artichoke hearts. Pat dry and cut into quarters. Chop parsley.

In a 12 inch skillet cook garlic in oil and butter over moderate heat, stirring until fragrant. Add artichokes and cook, stirring, until heated through. Stir in roasted peppers, parsley, remaining ingredients and salt and pepper to taste. Serve at room temperature with crusty bread.

Delicious Artichoke Dip

1/2 cup mayonnaise
1/2 cup sour cream
1 cup grated Parmesan cheese
1 can artichoke hearts, drained
1/2 cup minced onion
1 tbsp. lemon juice
salt and pepper to taste

Preheat oven to 400 F. Stir together mayo, cream, cheese and onion. Mix in artichoke hearts, lemon juice, salt and pepper. In a shallow baking dish, bake at 400 degrees for 20 minutes until light brown on top.

Sally R's Scrumptious Peanut Butter Bars

2 sticks softened butter
1/2 cup peanut butter
2 cups packed light brown sugar
2 eggs
2.5 tsp. vanilla extract
2.5 cups quick-cook rolled oats
2.5 cups all-purpose flour
1 tsp. baking soda
1/2 tsp. salt
2/3 cup cocoa powder
1/4 cup granulated sugar
1 can sweetened condensed milk (14 oz.)
3/4 cup Reese's Pieces
1/2 cup mini peanut butter cups (or 1.5 cups Reese's Baking Cups - crushed

Dough Prep
Preheat oven to 350 F. Beat one stick butter with PB and brown sugar until fluffy (in electric mixer). Add eggs and 1 tsp. vanilla extract. Mix until combined.

In a separate bowl, combine oats, flour, baking soda and salt. Gradually combine oat mixture with butter mixture (it will be thick).

Set aside 2 cups of dough and press remaining dough into an ungreased 15.5 x 10.5 x 1 inch pan.

Filling Prep
Melt the remaining stick of butter over medium heat Stir in cocoa and granulated sugar. Add the can of milk into the mixture and stir until thick and shiny. Remove from heat and stir in 1.5 tsp. vanilla extract. Spread mixture evenly over the dough in the pan. Sprinkle the crushed Reese's Pieces cups over the chocolate mix. Crumble the reserved dough evenly over the Reese's cups.

Bake for 25-30 minutes or until top is golden brown. Cool completely in the pan. Cut into bars and enjoy!

Fun Bat Fact: Bats are strong allies in orchards, controlling night-flying pests, such as the codling moth which preys on a variety of crops, including apples.

Enjoy the following apple recipes made possible by bats.

Tabatha's Apple Fritters

1/2 cup milk
1 tsp. vanilla extract
1 egg
2 tbsp. butter, melted and cooled
1 tbsp. baking powder
1/4 tsp. salt
1.5 cups cake flour
1 tbs. orange zest
1/2 cups chopped apples, skins on
1/2 cup sugar
apple butter (optional)
vegetable oil for frying

Preheat 2 to 3 inches of oil in a deep fryer to 375 degrees. Blend first four ingredients. In a separate bowl, combine baking powder, salt and flour with a wire whisk. Fold flour, zest and apples into wet mixture. Drop spoons-full of batter into hot oil. Fry for about 2-3 minutes or until golden brown. Drain on paper towels. Lightly toss with sugar. Serve warm with apple butter if desired.

Red's Apple Butter

 4 lbs of mixed cooking apples (skins on), cored, and cut into large chunks
1 cup apple cider
1 cup brown sugar
2 tablespoons lemon juice
1 teaspoon ground cinnamon
1/4 teaspoon ground nutmeg
1/8 teaspoon ground cloves
1/8 teaspoons ground allspice

 Place apple and apple cider in a large heavy pot and bring to a simmer over medium heat. Cover and cook until apples are completely tender, about 20 to 30 minutes.

Place half of the apples in a large metal sieve and make a puree. The skins will remain in the sieve. Pour into a medium bowl and repeat with remaining apples.

Pour puréed apples back into large pot and simmer over medium-low heat. Stir in sugar, lemon juice, cinnamon, nutmeg, cloves, and allspice. Continue to simmer, uncovered, until sauce turns a deep reddish-brown and thickens, about 1 to 2 hours, stirring regularly to prevent burning.

 Let apple butter cool to room temperature, then store in an airtight container in the refrigerator for up to three weeks.

Boris' Bread & Butter Pickles - refrigerator method

3 pounds pickling cucumbers
3 large sweet onions, thinly sliced
1/2 cup Kosher salt
1 1/2 cups sugar
1 1/2 cups white vinegar
3/4 teaspoon turmeric
3 Tablespoons mustard seeds
3 Tablespoons coriander seeds
3/4 teaspoon celery seed

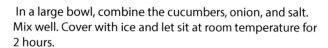

In a large bowl, combine the cucumbers, onion, and salt. Mix well. Cover with ice and let sit at room temperature for 2 hours.

In a large pot, bring the sugar, vinegar and spices to a boil. Drain the cucumber mixture, add to the vinegar mixture and bring almost to a boil. Remove from the heat and let cool. Store in an airtight container for up to 3 weeks in the fridge. They will start to get that pickled flavor after a few hours, but allow more time for the full effect.

Pippy's Pickled Green Tomatoes

1 pound green tomatoes, stemmed and cut into wedges
1/2 cup white vinegar
1/2 cup water
1 1/2 teaspoons pickling salt
2 teaspoons dill seed
4 garlic cloves
1/2 teaspoon peppercorn
2 bay leaves

Place the following into the bottom of a hot canning jar:
1 teaspoon dill seed
2 garlic cloves
1/4 teaspoon peppercorn
1 bay leaf

Combine vinegar, water and salt and bring to a boil. Pack tomato wedges into the jars. Pour brine slowly into the jars. Use a wooden chopstick to remove the air bubbles and add a bit of additional brine if necessary. Wipe rims, and apply sterilized lids and screw on bands.

Process in a boiling water canner for 10 minutes. When time is up, remove jars from canner and let them cool on a towel-lined counter top. When jars are completely cool, remove rings and test seals by grasping the edges of the lid and lifting the jar. If the lids hold fast, the seal is good. Store in a cool, dark place for up to one year. Pickles are good to eat after one week of curing.

Jack O's Creamy-Spicy Pumpkin Soup

1 Tbs. oil
1 small onion, sliced
2 gloves garlic - chopped or pressed
1 Tbsp. grated fresh ginger
1 Tbsp. corriander (ground seed)
1 tsp. cinnamon
1/4 tsp. nutmeg
pinch cayenne pepper
1/2 cup dry white wine
1 16 oz. can pumpkin *
1 cup half-and-half
2 cups vegetable broth (can use boullion)
1 to 2 tsp. sugar
Parmesan or cheddar cheese (optional)

In a large pot or saucepan, heat oil and saute onions until soft. Add garlic and ginger and cook for another 30 seconds, then add the spices for another 30 seconds until fragrant - do not let the spices burn. Add wine, stir for a minute or so, and remove from heat.

Add the pumpkin and one cup of liquid. Puree with a stick blender or food processor. When smooth, heat in the pot with the rest of the liquid simmering.

Taste. Add a small amount of sugar. Add a small amount of hot sauce or raw grated ginger for more of a kick. Garnish with grated Parmesan or sharp cheddar cheese.

*If using fresh pumpkin, place the pumpkin on a baking sheet, slit it to let out the steam, and cook in a 350 F oven until soft - about 45 to 60 minutes. Split, let cool, and scoop out the seeds and pulp. Mash or use a blender until the puree is smooth.

Arturo's Sauce Picante (Yield: one cup)

1/4 cup finely chopped mushrooms
1/4 cup water
1/4 cup tomato sauce
1/4 cup cider vinegar
1 Tbsp. brown sugar
1/2 tsp. salt
1 large garlic clove - finely chopped
1/4 tsp. black pepper
pinch ginger - pinch nutmeg
dash hot pepper (optional)

Mix ingredients together and cook slowly until it bubbles.

Great as a topping for open-faced grilled cheese sandwiches.

Maggie O's Tomato Cobbler

Filling
3 Tbsp. unsalted butter
1 medium onion, diced
2 cloves garlic, minced
1 tsp. chopped fresh thyme
1/8 tsp. cayenne pepper
3 large tomatoes cut into chunks
1 tsp. packed light brown sugar
Kosher salt
2 cups cherry tomatoes, halved
3 tbsp. all-purpose flour

Topping
1 1/2 cups all-purpose flour
1 1/2 tsp. baking powder
1 tsp. granulated sugar
Kosher salt and black pepper
6 Tbsp. cold unsalted butter, thinly sliced
2/3 cups milk, plus more for brushing
2 tsp. whole-grain mustard
1 tsp. chopped fresh thyme

Preheat oven to 350 F. Make the filling. Heat 2 tablespoons butter in a large skillet over medium-high heat. Add the onion and cook until soft, golden brown. Add the garlic, thyme and cayenne and cook one more minute. Add the chopped tomatoes, brown sugar and 1 1/4 teaspoons salt. Bring to a simmer and cook until the tomatoes just begin to soften. Remove from heat, then gently stir in cherry tomatoes and flour. Transfer to a 2 quart baking dish and dot with remaining 1 tablespoon butter.

Make the topping: Whisk flour, baking powder, granulated sugar, 3/4 teaspoon salt, and black pepper to taste in a medium bowl. Add the butter and use a pastry cutter or fingers to rub the butter into the flour until it resembles coarse meal with pea-size pieces of butter. Add the milk, mustard and thyme and gently mix with a fork just until a sticky dough forms, being careful not to overwork the dough.

Drop balls of dough over the tomato filling and brush with milk. Place the cobbler on a baking sheet and bake until golden and bubbling, about an hour. Let rest for 15 min. before serving.

Sweet Bat Fact: Because free-tailed bats' wings and echo-location characteristics are adapted to feeding over open spaces, they are excellent candidates for providing insect pest control over fields of sugarcane.
(BATS magazine)

Red's Spicy Lentil Soup

2 Tablespoons olive oil
1 onion, chopped
3 cloves garlic, minced
7 carrots, chopped
1 teaspoon cumin
1 teaspoon turmeric
2 teaspoon coriander
1/2 teaspoon paprika
1/4 teaspoon cinnamon
6 cups vegetable broth
1-15 oz can diced tomatoes
2 cups cooked red lentils, rinsed until water runs clear Salt and pepper to taste. Sauté the onion and garlic in olive oil until soft. Add carrots and sauté until carrots are tender about 10-12 minutes.

Add spices and sauté for an additional 2 minutes.
Add broth, tomatoes and lentils and stir to combine.
Simmer on low heat for about 30 minutes until lentils are tender. Blend soup to make it creamy.

Garnish with a dollop of Greek yogurt, chopped fresh cilantro (or parsley), red pepper flakes and fresh lemon juice.

Gingered Fig & Cranberry Chutney with Walnuts (BCI)

12 ounces fresh cranberries
¼ cup onion, minced
1 cup light brown sugar
½ cup orange juice
½ cup apple cider vinegar
¼ cup raisins
8 dried black mission figs, cut into eighths
1 Tbsp. fresh ginger, finely minced
½ tsp. ground cinnamon
½ tsp. red pepper flakes
1/3 cup walnuts, toasted and roughly chopped

Add all the ingredients, with the exception of the chopped walnuts, to a medium pot and bring to a boil. Lower the heat to bring the mix to a simmer, and cook for 20-25 minutes, stirring occasionally, until the chutney thickens some. Remove from the heat, stir in the nuts and let cool slightly before serving. Serves 12-15.

Fun Bat Fact: The Amazon fruit bat's eating habits help deposit fig trees seeds and also ensure that seedling will sprout far enough from the parent tree that they do not have to compete for root space and soil nutrients.

We hope you enjoy these wonderful recipes
brought to you by bats.

Now it's time for us to fly.

Goodbye!

Fun Bat Facts

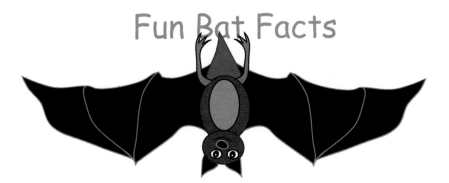

- Bats are the only mammals that truly fly.

- Roughly 1/4 of all mammal species are bats.

- Bats date back 50 million years to the Eocine era.

- Bats are not birds.

- Bats are not flying mice. They are *chiroptera,* which means *hand-wing*

- A bat's wing has four fingers and a thumb, just like a person's hand.

- Bats are not blind, but they use *echolocation* to find food at night.

- Echolocation is a type of sonar that lets bats "see with their ears."

- Don't worry: the last thing a bat wants is to get tangled in your hair.

- Bats are not mean or vicious, but they *are* wild animals and might bite if handled and frightened. *Never* pick up a grounded bat!

- Most mother bats give birth to only one baby (pup) each year.

- If you leave bats alone, they'll do the same for you - and provide many services safely and effectively - free of charge!

Made in the USA
Middletown, DE
09 October 2022